101

WAYS TO

SPEAK

IN FRONT OF

YOUR WHOLE

CLASS

With No Fear!

101

WAYS TO

SPEAK

IN FRONT OF

YOUR WHOLE

CLASS

With No Fear!

by Steve Anthony
illustrated by Aija Janums

To my brother, Dave,
who is never at a loss for words
—S. A.

CONTENTS

Chapter 1

So Who Wants to Speak in Public Anyway?

Public speaking—for most people, no two words are guaranteed to send more chills down the spine. Among our fears, speaking in public has to be near the top of the list. In fact, some of us would rather face a hungry grizzly bear than a roomful of people!

Let me tell you a little secret. Speaking well and confidently in public is something you can learn, just like your ABCs or the multiplication tables. It's a skill that can be developed through preparation and practice.

Wait a minute, you say. Who wants to speak in public anyway? Certainly not me. I wouldn't volunteer to get up and talk before a group in a million years. So just forget it! I'm very happy to sit back and let someone else do it.

Fair enough. But before you shut this book, let me give you three good reasons why improving your public speaking skills is important—no matter who you are.

Public speaking is something you will not be able to avoid as a student. If your teacher hasn't already assigned an oral report on a book or a topic, he or she will do so soon. At one time or another, you will also probably have to demonstrate or present something to the class. It might be a cooking recipe, a science experiment, or a craft. *That's* public speaking, too.

Then there are speeches. Maybe you'd like to run for Student Council or class president. You will need to make a short speech about why your classmates should vote for you. Or maybe as a member of a club or an organization you will have to introduce a guest, present an award, or accept an honor.

So, you see, public speaking is something you're going to have to face—like it or not. Since you are going to have to deal with it, you might as well prepare yourself to do your best.

If you do the job well, you'll improve your grade, gain some self-confidence, and possibly win the admiration of your classmates. You may even find yourself becoming a leader among your peers instead of a follower—someone people rely on to give an opinion, communicate ideas, and express concerns.

I did say there were *three* reasons, didn't I? The other two reasons may not mean much to you now, but they will in the years ahead. Good speaking, like good writing, helps you express feelings and ideas so you can communicate them clearly to others. It will make you a fuller, more interesting, and ultimately more satisfied person.

The third reason is perhaps the strongest. Whatever career you pursue after your school years, public speaking definitely will be an asset.

Some jobs, such as politician, clergyman, actor, and television or radio broadcaster require good public speaking skills. But the ability to speak well and express yourself is useful in just about any kind of work you choose. It will come in handy when you have to address a group of people at work, share your ideas in an office meeting, or simply communicate daily with your boss and co-workers.

Who wants to speak in public? The answer to this critical question is, you do! The little book you're holding right now can help you get started. So turn the page and keep reading!

Chapter 2

Butterflies in Your Stomach— Stage Fright

It's your worst nightmare.

You're standing on a stage. A fat microphone is staring you in the face. Bright lights are blinding you, and there, beyond the lights, is a sea of unfriendly faces. A million people are looking up at you, waiting for you to speak. You open your mouth, but nothing comes out. You try to speak, but your vocal chords are paralyzed. Your mouth is as dry as sawdust, and your heart is racing like a car at the Indy 500.

What you're going through is a bad case of stage fright. In this chapter we'll tell you what stage fright is, and we'll give you some tips to help you conquer your fears.

1. The dictionary defines stage fright as a condition of extreme nervousness experienced by a speaker or an actor.

2. Stage fright is the greatest obstacle that most of us face when we attempt to speak in public. It can affect every kind of public speaking, so let's face it right at the start of this book. Before we go any further, there are three important things you should know about stage fright.

3. Almost everyone gets nervous before speaking. Even the most accomplished speakers and actors readily admit that they get butterflies in the stomach before they step out in front of an audience. Being nervous in this situation is normal and very human. No one's immune to it. Don't feel alone, because you have lots of company.

4. It's good to be nervous! Any professional actor or athlete will tell you it's okay to be nervous before you perform in public. It means you're "up," alert, and ready to go. It means you have the extra energy needed to do a great job. If you were totally laid back and fully relaxed, you probably would not do so well. It's only when the nervousness gets out of control and stage fright sets in that problems arise. Learning to control and channel your nervousness is one of the keys to becoming a good public speaker.

5. Stage fright is actually a state of mind. The manifestations of stage fright are physical—dry mouth, butterflies in your stomach, and clammy hands, to name a few—but it all begins in your head. It's not failure that you fear, but the fear of failure—of making a fool of yourself before all those people. Believe it or not, those people out there want to like you, and they want you to succeed. They're on *your* side. The fear you feel is only an illusion, but if you let it run wild it can sink your speech. Here's what you must do, *before* you begin speaking, to make sure your speech is a success.

6. Be prepared. This is the Boy Scouts' motto, and it should be yours, too. It's only common sense that the more prepared you are, the less afraid you'll be of messing up. Being prepared means not only knowing what you're going to say, but also deciding in advance of your speech what visual aids you'll use, being familiar with the space where you'll be speaking, and having all other aspects of your presentation under control.

7. Practice makes perfect. Go over your speech or talk—not once, but several times. Say it to your mirror at home. Give a dress rehearsal to members of your family or a good friend. This will serve two purposes. First, it will get you used to speaking in front of others, so you'll be less nervous when you face your audience. Second, your first audience can make constructive suggestions on how you might improve your speech. Listen to these suggestions and use the ones that make sense to you. Then give your speech again to the same people. Practice may not always make perfect, but it will improve your speech and give you the confidence you need to succeed.

8. Don't memorize your speech. There are times when someone needs to memorize a speech, but you, a beginner, shouldn't try it. Memorizing takes a lot of effort, and the chances that you'll mess up somewhere along the line are great. If you lose your train of thought and can't remember what to say next, you could be paralyzed by stage fright. It's much wiser to know what you're going to say reasonably well and jot down the main points on 3 x 5 index cards. They will fit easily in your hand, and you can take them up to the podium with you. Refer to them when necessary. With the cards prompting you to the next idea, you will be free to look at your audience, to speak easily and conversationally, and to make a good impression on your listeners.

9. Be familiar with the space. An unfamiliar environment can be unnerving to even the most experienced public speakers. You may not have any problem speaking in your classroom, but if you are speaking in a place you don't know, try to arrive early

so you can look around. Become familiar with where you'll be standing and where your audience will be sitting. Go to the front of the room and look out at the empty seats. Imagine them filled with people eager to hear what you have to say. The more comfortable you are with the space, the less nervous you'll be when the time comes to speak.

10. If you need to use a microphone, try it out ahead of time. Many speakers are mike shy. That is, they don't feel comfortable hearing their voice boom back at them from loud speakers. But sometimes you have to use a mike to be heard.

When properly used, a microphone can be a speaker's best friend rather than worst enemy. If you'll need to use a microphone, try to test it out ahead of time to figure out how loudly you'll have to speak and how far away from the mike you'll need to stand. Then make any necessary adjustments to a stationary mike so you'll feel comfortable speaking into it. The microphone should be a little below your chin so it doesn't hide your face, but make sure it isn't so low that you'll need to bend over to speak.

11. Relax! You're about to step up to speak, and the butterflies inside your stomach are beating their wings double time. If you feel as though you're about to faint, try some of the stress-relieving techniques on pages 20–21.

12. Take a drink. Many speaker's platforms are equipped with a water pitcher and a glass. Talking for any length of time dries the throat and makes it hard to talk. If you're nervous before standing up to speak, you may already be experiencing "dry mouth." There may not be a pitcher handy, so take a swallow of water from a fountain as close to the time of your speech as possible. It will lubricate your throat and refresh you. Now you're ready to face your audience.

STRESS-RELIEVING
TECHNIQUES TO TRY

Stage fright is often a gut reaction to fear, and it manifests itself physically. You can relieve the physical symptoms of stage fright by using the following physical techniques. Try each one to see which works best for you.

Breathe deeply. This is usually a surefire stress buster. Take a big, deep breath slowly in through your nose with your mouth shut. Hold the breath for a count of four. Then let it out slowly through your mouth. Repeat this exercise two or three times. You'll be amazed how relaxed and calm you'll feel.

Tighten and relax body muscles. Tighten your muscles to relax them? It really works. Tense all of the muscles in one area of your body for a count of four and then relax them completely. You can start with your feet and work your way up—legs, backside, chest, neck, face, and forehead. By the time you finish, your whole body should feel refreshed.

Stretch! We stretch when we wake up in the morning or when we're tired or tense. It gets the muscles moving and the blood pumping. Put your arms up above your head and stretch them as far as you can. Stretch your neck and slowly rotate your head. Feels good, doesn't it?

Visualization. This technique is more mental than physical, but it works for many people. Try picturing pleasant and positive images in your head—a favorite pastime, a beautiful landscape, a person or pet you really care about. This "mind over matter" exercise will put you in good spirits and boost your confidence.

A different approach to this technique is to picture bad things—war scenes, natural disasters, or a personal memory of a difficult situation. The idea is that by thinking about these bad experiences, you'll put the present situation into perspective—and you'll realize that, however scary giving your speech may seem to you, it's nothing to worry about if you look at the big picture.

There's one popular visualization technique that many people swear by—imagine every member of your audience is sitting there without a stitch of clothing on. This is supposed to make you feel superior and boost your confidence. Give it a try, but be careful not to laugh out loud!

13. Look at your audience. Some people are afraid to look at the audience because they think eye contact will give them stage fright. But if you don't look up at the people you're speaking to, so you can see how they are reacting to you, you're liable to become even more nervous. More important, you need to connect with your audience to keep them interested in what you have to say.

If looking directly at people distracts you, focus on a point at the back of the room or fix your gaze on a sympathetic face in the crowd and talk directly to that person. Perhaps you can ask a good friend or a relative to sit close to the front so you can look at him or her if you get nervous. Try different techniques and see which works best for you. With time and a little practice it will seem natural to look out at your audience while you speak.

14. Break the ice with a joke. Humor is a great stress reliever and a sure way to capture the full attention of the audience. That's why so many clergymen try to start off their sermons with a funny joke or entertaining story. You can do the same, telling a brief joke or funny line near the start of your speech. You don't have to be Jerry Seinfeld to get a laugh, but you do need to make sure your joke is truly a funny one that your listeners will appreciate. If you don't know any jokes, ask your friends for suggestions or go to the library and read some joke books.

People listening to a public speaker are eager to offer encouragement to that speaker, and one way they can do that is through laughter. It puts them at ease and will put you at ease, too. The sound of laughter will clear your head and boost your confidence. You might even make a joke about your own nervousness.

Example: "I'd rather be sitting in detention right now than standing here in front of you."

Just remember, one joke is usually enough! It's meant as an ice breaker. Now get on with your speech.

15. Be aware of nervous mannerisms. When speakers are nervous they tend to do strange things with their bodies, without even noticing it—like tapping a foot, blinking their eyes, or shifting weight from one foot to the other. You may not know that you're doing these things, but your audience surely will. The distraction will shift their attention away from your carefully prepared presentation. Try to stay still, poised but relaxed. When you practice your speech, ask your friend or family member to alert you to any distracting movements you make. Once you are conscious of these nervous tics, and if you are really involved in what you're saying, your nervousness should disappear and so should any distracting movements.

16. One way to avoid nervous mannerisms is to keep your hands busy. Holding index cards will give you something to do with your hands. Or you may hold a pen or pencil in one hand. Gesturing during your speech can help make a point and use up some of that nervous energy in a constructive way, but your hands shouldn't be moving constantly. It's okay to take a few steps across the stage occasionally, but don't wander around so much that your movements distract the audience.

17. If something unexpected happens, don't panic. No matter how prepared you are, things may happen over which you have no control—a faulty microphone or sound system, a jet roaring overhead in the middle of your speech, a sudden announcement over the PA system, a visual aid that falls to the floor. Even if your audience laughs or becomes distracted, don't let these interruptions throw you. But don't act like nothing has happened, either. If there's a disruptive noise, stop talking and wait until it passes. If you drop something, pick it up and continue. If the sound system needs to be fixed, wait while someone else corrects the problem. You might, if you wish, make a good-humored comment about the interruption, but don't dwell on it. Take it in stride and get on with your speech as soon as possible.

18. Most important of all, have fun! Public speaking should be viewed not as a punishment, but as an opportunity—a chance to show off your knowledge, communicate with others, and (yes!) enjoy yourself. Just as stage fright is a state of mind, so is being an effective public speaker. If you believe in yourself, so will your audience. Stage fright, like so many of our fears, is irrational. Once you master it, you'll find speaking in public isn't really so bad after all. In fact, it can even be fun!

Chapter 3

Speaking in the Classroom: Oral Reports

An oral report is the presentation—through speech—of information about a particular topic. During the school year, your teacher may assign a number of oral reports on different topics in different subject areas—a famous writer in language arts; a country or an ethnic group in social studies; a famous scientist or an environmental issue in science. The topic may be a person, a country, an animal, a scientific discovery, a social issue, or just about anything that relates to your schoolwork.

Your teacher may ask you to prepare a written version of your report, but the main requirement will be that you deliver it orally to the class—probably within a certain time limit. The teacher may assign the topic or you may be asked to choose one.

19. If you have a choice, pick a topic that genuinely interests you. It may be a favorite animal, a favorite book, or something or someone you've always wanted to know more about. If you are assigned a topic that doesn't interest you, ask your teacher if you can switch to a different topic. Your boredom will come across in your oral report, and your audience won't be interested either. If, however, you are enthusiastic in your presentation, your excitement will spread to the audience—and your report will be a smashing success.

20. If you can't think of a good topic, ask your teacher for help. Your teacher wants you to do your best with your assignment, so he or she is probably more than willing to offer some suggestions. Try to be as specific as possible when you speak to your teacher about things that interest you. If you're still stuck, a parent or older sibling, or someone else who knows you well, might have some good ideas. You can also review what you've learned in school. By going over your notes and looking through your textbooks, you should be able to find an interesting topic for your report, one that is especially suited to your class. Or read newspapers and news magazines to find a topic in current events that you and your audience will find interesting.

21. Choose a topic that fits your needs. You want to be able to cover your topic as thoroughly as possible in the allotted time, which is usually between three and ten minutes. If your topic is too big, you won't have time to touch on all the key points, and your report won't be effective. If the topic is too small, you'll run out of things to say before the time is up. Narrow or widen your topic to fit the time requirement. For example, the topic of African Americans in the early West is too broad for a short oral report. By narrowing it down to one group of African-Americans in the West, such as the black cowboys or buffalo soldiers, you have a manageable topic that suits your assignment.

22. Pick a topic about which you can find enough information. Suppose you are asked to focus on one particular black cowboy for your oral report. You will want to choose one about whom you can gather enough information to make your report comprehensive and interesting. Say you do some preliminary research and then narrow your topic down to two black cowboys—outlaw Cherokee Bill and rodeo champion Bill Pickett. At your library you discover very little information about Cherokee Bill, but you find two biographies on Bill Pickett. The better choice for your report would be Bill Pickett.

23. Every oral report must have a purpose. There are three main reasons for giving a report: to inform, to persuade, or to entertain. Knowing your purpose in advance will help you shape your report to fulfill its purpose.

- A report that informs gives knowledge about a topic and helps people understand it.

- A persuasive report tries to convince the audience that the speaker's opinion about a subject or issue is the best one.

- A report that entertains is meant to amuse or move an audience through funny or interesting stories and anecdotes.

Even if your primary purpose is to inform, you may add an entertaining story or two about your topic to persuade your listeners to view the information in a certain way. Decide what your main purpose will be and make sure your report fulfills it.

24. Research your topic at the library. Books, almanacs, encyclopedias, magazines, and newspapers are all good sources for information about most topics. (Some topics, such as personal ones based on your own experiences, won't require this kind of research, although you may still want to use the library to gather some background information about your topic.) Ask the librarian to help you locate these materials. He or she may also know of other sources that can provide additional information. Don't be afraid to ask for help!

25. Don't forget to check out the Internet, too. The Internet has a wealth of material on many topics. If your home computer isn't "on line," find out if you can access the Internet on computers at your school or library. Just remember that anyone can create a web site and that the information you find there may not be entirely accurate. The facts you use in your report should come from a reliable source, such as one of those listed in tip 24, above, or from Internet sites maintained by reputable organizations.

26. Seek out other sources of information besides printed matter. You might find a great video that relates to your topic, or a CD, or even an expert you can interview. For example, if your report is on the history of your community, you might arrange to interview an elderly neighbor who has lived all her life on your block. She will be able to give you the kind of personal, first-hand information you can't get from a book.

27. Take good notes. Careful note-taking is a critical part of research. Without it, how will you remember all the key points of what you've read? Here are some guidelines for good note-taking.

1. Write your notes in a spiral-bound notebook so they will be all together in one, easy-to-find place.

2. Take lots of notes. You can always weed out the information you don't need later. Better to have more information on your topic than not enough.

3. Remember to write down all of the sources from which you gathered information. You may need to support the facts of your oral report by citing your sources. Also, if your teacher wants a written version of your report, you'll need to list these sources in a bibliography. Look on pages 84–87 for more information about bibliographies.

28. Develop an outline. After you have finished your research, you will want to organize your notes into a structure for your oral report. In an outline, you can list the main points you want to make about your topic and the details that support them. The outline, and your report, will consist of three main parts: an introduction, a body, and a conclusion.

Here is a sample outline for an oral report on Bill Pickett:

A. Introduction
  1. Bill Pickett was a great rodeo star and cowboy
  2. His specialty was bulldogging
  3. Others used their hands, Bill used his teeth

Body

B. Pickett's unique style of bulldogging
  1. He grabbed a steer and bit into its underlip
  2. This made him a star in the 1901 Wild West Show

C. Bill was a hit in New York City
  1. He bulldogged a runaway steer in Madison Square Garden
  2. He was helped by future cowboy star Will Rogers

D. Traveled with show to England
  1. Appeared before the King and Queen
  2. World War I broke out, Wild West show returned to U.S.

E. Last years of Bill Pickett
  1. Retired from rodeo and became a gentleman rancher
  2. Died trying to rope a horse that kicked him in the head

F. Conclusion
  1. Bill Pickett was greatest bulldogger of all
  2. Remembered in the Cowboy Hall of Fame
  3. Pictured on a U.S. postage stamp

29. The introduction should introduce your topic and say something interesting about it. Your goal is to grab the audience's attention early so they'll want to hear the rest of your report. To do that, you must use your imagination. Work in an unusual fact about your topic, an intriguing teaser that will make the audience want to know more, or something interesting that somebody said about the subject. The following examples illustrate all three techniques:

An unusual fact

Bill Pickett, black rodeo champ, has been dead for more than sixty years, but you might come face-to-face with him the next time you mail a letter. Bill Pickett is the only black cowboy who has been pictured on a U.S. postage stamp.

An intriguing teaser

Bill Pickett was the greatest bulldogger of all time. Other bulldoggers pulled down a steer with their hands. Bill relied on a secret weapon—his teeth.

Bill Pickett's friend and boss, Zack Miller, once said that Bill was the "greatest sweat-and-dirt cowboy who ever lived." Pickett's achievements as a rodeo star support this opinion.

30. The body of your report should give information about your topic in an organized fashion. Each main point listed in your outline should be preceded by a capital letter and each supporting detail by a number, as in the sample outline on page 33. Choose the most important or interesting information from your notes for the body of your presentation.

31. The conclusion summarizes the main points of your report and should arrive at some conclusion about the topic.

Example: "Bill Pickett was a great cowboy and rodeo performer. He perfected the event of bulldogging, raising it to a fine art. He was the first black cowboy elected to the Cowboy Hall of Fame and is pictured on a postage stamp. His legacy lives on today."

32. Write out your report based on your outline if your teacher requires it. If your teacher doesn't want a written report, you may still find it helpful to go through this extra step prior to making your oral presentation. By doing so, you may remember the main points of your report better and improve your oral delivery.

33. Don't, however, read your written report. In Chapter 2, you learned why you shouldn't try to memorize your report. Reading during your presentation is not a good idea either. You will spend most of your time looking down at a sheet of paper and not up at your audience. Also, unless you are experienced at reading aloud, you may stumble over your words or become monotonous. Your listeners will get bored, and your report will be less effective.

34. Instead, write the main ideas from your outline or written report on 3 x 5 index cards. These are small and will fit easily into your hand. You can refer to the cards as you give your oral report. Write down only a few words or a phrase that you can glance at quickly to prompt your memory. The following example shows how the first part of the body from the outline on Bill Pickett might look on an index card:

B. Bulldogging Style
1. most bulldoggers pulled down with hands
2. Bill bit into upper lip
3. made him star of 1901 Wild West Show

These are the bare bones. You should know your topic well enough to speak spontaneously and fill in many other details from memory. Note that in the sample report, the word "bulldogger" needs to be defined by the speaker. Whatever your topic, make sure you explain any key words with which the audience might not be familiar.

35. Look for places in your report where you can add audio or visual aids. These tools can bring your report to life and make it more understandable to your audience. For example, if you're talking about Bill Pickett, you might show a photograph of him on his horse or display a copy of a poster advertising his Wild West Show. Other visual aids you might use include diagrams, models, graphs, charts, flip charts, slides, and words written out on a chalkboard. Audio aids include records, audio cassettes, and CDs of music and the spoken word. A good audio aid for a report on Bill Pickett might be to play part of a cowboy song, especially one having to do with bulldogging. You might open or close your report with the recording to set the mood.

36. Practice your oral report by yourself and before a few friends or family members. This was mentioned in Chapter 2, but it's worth repeating. You might also record your report on an audio cassette and listen to your voice. If you are speaking too softly, you'll need to talk more loudly to be heard. If you tend to mumble or swallow words, you'll need to work on speaking more clearly. If you are talking too fast, make a conscious effort to slow down. Volume, diction, and pace are all terribly important. If your audience can't hear and understand what you're saying, your report will not be successful—no matter how great your topic is. Ask others to be honest with you about your delivery and take their comments seriously, so you can make any necessary adjustments before you actually give your report.

37. Get a good night's sleep the night before. You'll want to be at your best for your oral report, just like you'd want to be well rested for a sports event or a test.

38. Dress appropriately. Wear clothes that are neat but comfortable. Make sure you look your best—comb your hair, brush your teeth, and check to make sure your hands and nails are clean. You don't want your appearance to distract from your presentation. For a dramatic touch, you might wear a piece of clothing suggestive of your subject—a cowboy hat for an oral report on Bill Pickett, for example. Be inventive.

39. Make sure everyone can see your visual aids. Don't get in the way of a visual aid. Your audience will be frustrated and distracted if they can't see it. Make sure all of your props are large enough for everyone to see. For example, most people in an audience wouldn't be able to see a picture of Bill Pickett on a postage stamp. But everyone would be able to see a blown-up picture of the stamp. Don't pass around visual aids unless your teacher asks you to. While people are examining the visual aid, they won't be listening to you.

40. Do a final check before you begin. Look over your index cards one last time. Make sure you have all the visual and audio aids you'll be using and that you know how to operate any necessary equipment, such as an overhead projector. Take a drink of water before you begin to avoid "dry mouth." Review the Oral Report Checklist on pages 78–80 at the back of this book for other helpful last-minute tips.

41. Take your time. Once you've started presenting your oral report, pace yourself. Most people tend to speak fast when they are nervous. Be conscious of this and try to slow down. Pause briefly between sentences. Speak clearly and distinctly. Give your audience plenty of time to see your visual aids and to hear your audio aids.

42. Cut out all the "ums," "ahs," and "you knows." Repetitive speech mannerisms can drive an audience crazy—the same effect that a tapping foot can have. Ask a friend or relative to count the number of times you use one of these words or sounds as you practice your speech. Then consciously work on editing them out of your oral delivery. Using these words is a bad habit that can easily be broken once you're aware of it.

43. When you finish speaking, answer any questions. The teacher may have a few questions for you or may expect you to answer questions from the entire class, so don't run back to your seat after you finish speaking! Answer each question succinctly and to the best of your ability. If you don't know an answer, don't be afraid to say so. That's much better than trying to bluff your way through and getting caught doing it. If your teacher seems especially interested in something you're not sure about, offer to do a little more research and find the answer. You'll benefit by learning a bit more about your topic, and your teacher will appreciate the extra effort.

44. Before you leave the speaker's area, be sure you take everything you brought with you. Don't forget your index cards or your audio and visual aids, especially if someone else is giving an oral report right after you.

Chapter 4

Show and Tell: Presentations and Demonstrations

Remember when you were in kindergarten and you had "show and tell" at the beginning of the school day? You got to bring something from home into class—a pet, a toy, or perhaps something you made—and to tell your classmates about it. You didn't know it at the time, but this was probably your first experience with public speaking.

Now that you're older, you're still doing "show and tell," although you may not think of it that way. Instead of showing the class a toy, you might be talking about a poster you made in art class, an invention or display for a science fair, or a recipe for a favorite snack. No matter what your presentation is about, this chapter is filled with great ideas for making it the best it can be.

45. Oral presentations and demonstrations differ from oral reports in that they include showing as much as telling about something. Presentations and demonstrations often involve showing how to do something or describing how something works. Perhaps your presentation will be in your classroom, but it might just as easily be in the gym or an auditorium. It might be part of an event—such as an invention fair or a program devoted to colonial arts and crafts—that involves many other presentations.

46. Know the purpose of your presentation or demonstration. The purpose will usually be to inform your audience about a very specific subject. Remember that and don't allow yourself to become distracted and wander from your purpose by bringing in other topics or ideas.

47. Keep your presentation simple. No matter how complicated the thing or process you are explaining, you should try to simplify it as much as possible. Otherwise, your audience is going to get confused very quickly and lose track of what you are saying. Unfortunately, most people's listening skills are not as strong as their reading skills, so the simpler you keep your words, the better.

48. If you are describing a process, break it down into steps. Keep each step separate and distinct. Use order words, such as "first," "second," "then," "next," and "finally" before you begin speaking about each step in the process. You might even pause momentarily between steps. This will help your audience follow along and better understand your presentation.

49. Define any technical terms your audience may not recognize. Again, keep the definitions simple and to the point. If you need help understanding the meaning of a word, look in a dictionary or ask your teacher or a parent or older sibling for help.

50. Practice! Practice! Practice! Giving an oral presentation may seem more informal and therefore less stressful than giving an oral report, and in some ways it is. However, you will often be talking and pointing to visual aids or performing demonstrations at the same time. This can be difficult. If you mess up on one or the other, your presentation may suffer. To avoid this problem, practice your presentation over and over until it becomes second nature and you can talk easily while incorporating your props into your demonstration.

51. Make sure you have everything you need for your presentation or demonstration before you start. For example, you don't want to get to a step in your cooking demonstration and suddenly realize you don't have one of the most important ingredients for the recipe. Double-check all of your materials the night before and make sure you take everything with you in the morning.

52. Adjust the volume of your voice to your space. If you are presenting in a classroom, you can speak in a normal tone of voice. If, however, you are in a big hall at a science fair, and people are wandering from one display to another, you are going to have to speak more loudly to be heard over all the other noise around you. Speak loudly and clearly, but *never* strain your voice.

53. Be friendly and personable. This is especially important if you are speaking to small groups of people or individuals who are passing from one exhibit to another. You want to get their attention quickly and hold on to it until you're finished. Don't be offended if some people leave before the end of your demonstration. Depending on the number of different exhibits, not everyone may have the time or inclination to listen until the end of each one.

54. Involve your audience. It's always fun if you can get audience members directly involved in your presentation or demonstration. For example, if you are demonstrating a science experiment or a magic trick, call on a volunteer to assist you. Or, if you are cooking something, share the finished product with the audience so everyone can have a taste. (Get your teacher's permission before you do this.)

55. Answer any questions. People are more likely to have questions about a presentation than an oral report. Some people may even ask you questions before you're finished. If this is not appropriate or if interruptions bother you, politely ask the audience to hold their questions until you are done. If the questioner can't be heard by everyone, repeat the question before answering it. If you don't know the answer to a question, say so and direct the questioner to the teacher or someone else who may know the answer.

56. Relax and enjoy yourself! Presentations and demonstrations are usually more fun to do than oral reports, and your audience may be more interested and appreciative. And since you're actively doing something, you're less likely to be nervous. So have fun with your presentation or demonstration and enjoy sharing your knowledge and expertise with others.

Chapter 5

Speech! Speech!

A speech is a formal talk with a particular purpose given to a group of people. The president of a country addresses the nation. Your father gives a talk at his company's sales meeting. Your mother delivers a lecture to a group of professional women. A neighbor speaks out at a public meeting about a proposed mall project in your town. These are all speeches.

You probably think that speeches are grown-up stuff. A kid (especially you) would never be expected to give one, right? Think again. There are plenty of opportunities for you to give a speech. This chapter examines various kinds of speeches and gives you some tips on how to effectively deliver each one.

57. Kids can and do deliver speeches—and for some of the same reasons that adults do. For example, say you have a burning desire to run for president of your class at school or to become a member of the Student Council. You may have to give a *campaign speech* to let students know what you stand for and why they should vote for you. Now imagine that, by some twist of fate, you actually win the election. You'll probably have to give an *acceptance speech*.

Or maybe you win some kind of honor or award at school or outside of school. That's another acceptance speech. Or maybe someone else is getting an award and *you* are asked to introduce this person. Or perhaps someone famous is coming to talk at your school, and guess who gets picked to introduce him or her? That's an *introductory speech*.

Perhaps you're a member of your church or synagogue's youth group and you are asked to make an *announcement* about a group fund-raising activity during the worship service. That's a speech, too.

Or maybe there's an issue you feel strongly about that affects your school or neighborhood. You and a group of other people attend a town meeting to voice your *opinion*. You have a minute or two to express your opinion and gain support for your position. That's a short speech, but it's a speech nonetheless.

58. A speech is just another form of public speaking. Forget Lincoln's Gettysburg Address, John F. Kennedy's famous inaugural address, or Martin Luther King's stirring "I Have a Dream" speech. Your speech—just like thousands of speeches delivered by ordinary people each day—probably isn't going to be televised or written down in history books. But that doesn't mean your speech shouldn't be organized and well prepared. Most of the rules that apply to other kinds of public speaking apply to speeches, too, and if you follow many of the same suggestions presented earlier, there is no reason your speech won't be effective and successful.

59. A speech is usually voluntary. Unlike the oral reports and presentations you are required to give in school, a speech is generally not something you *have* to do in order to get a good grade. The point is, most people have a personal reason for giving a speech. In many instances there is something to be gained from it—perhaps you will get elected to office, receive an honor or award, get to honor someone else you admire, or persuade others to see your point of view and take some action on an issue about which you feel strongly. So you should feel enthusiastic about your topic and be really motivated to do the best job you can with your speech.

Here are five "Knows" you should keep in mind when you prepare and deliver your speech.

60. Know your purpose. Like oral reports, every speech has a purpose—to inform, to entertain, or to persuade. Nearly all opinions and campaign and political speeches are meant to persuade to some degree. Speeches meant primarily to entertain an audience are usually delivered by people called "after dinner speakers" or "toastmasters" and contain lots of jokes and funny stories. You probably won't be asked to give many of those until you're much older, if ever.

You may give a speech that informs in a simple way. An introductory speech, for instance, usually tells the audience who the person being introduced is and something about his or her background. Decide what the purpose of your speech is ahead of time and then gear everything you say to that purpose.

61. Know yourself. Know your strengths and weaknesses as a speaker. Maybe you're a natural-born storyteller, or maybe you can never remember the punch line to any joke—even right after you hear it. How good you are at telling stories and jokes should determine how much humor you inject into your speech. If you have a strong voice, use that asset to make your speech powerful. If you've acted in plays, use that sense of drama to bring your speech to life.

62. Know your audience. If you're speaking to a roomful of parents, you will probably talk more formally than if you are addressing a group of your peers. The audience at a sports banquet will expect you to talk about sports—a meeting of the Great Books Society will not. Always keep your audience in mind as you prepare your speech. If you are scheduled to speak to a group about which you know very little, do some research. Talk to a few members and find out some background information about the group. Details that are directly relevant to the audience will strengthen your speech, and your listeners will stay interested.

63. Know your space. You learned in Chapter 2 about familiarizing yourself with the speaker's area, but it's worth repeating here. Speeches are often given in places you haven't previously visited. Auditoriums and large halls can be scary and intimidating, even to professional speakers. The best way to overcome this feeling is to see the space where you're going to speak ahead of time, preferably before there's an audience in it. Walk around the stage area. Visualize how the seats will look filled with people. Try out the microphone if there is one. Get comfortable with your surroundings. When the time comes to speak, you will feel much more at ease and will be less likely to experience stage fright.

64. Know when to stop talking. We mentioned Lincoln's Gettysburg Address in Tip 58. It's the perfect example of a tight, well-written speech without a word wasted. Abraham Lincoln, one of the greatest speechwriters in American history, knew that brevity is a key to good speech-making. Audiences can forgive a speaker almost any failing, except being boring. Keep your speech reasonably short and to the point. Don't get sidetracked, don't repeat yourself, and leave 'em wanting more—not the other way around.

65. When giving a campaign speech, begin by grabbing the audience's attention. Most people have heard too many campaign speeches and don't look forward to hearing another one. If you want your classmates to listen to you, you've got to get their attention in a fresh and original way right at the start. You might begin with a touch of humor. ("I'm Brad Martin, and I never thought I'd want to be president of anything, until now.") Or you might open with a startling statistic or fact to introduce a campaign issue about which you feel strongly. ("Did you know that ninety percent of the schools in this state that have a uniform policy have less student crime and violence?") Being an attention grabber only works, of course, if you have something worthwhile to say after you've gotten everyone's attention. Make sure you do.

66. Take a position and state it clearly. You must provide a reason to make people feel inclined to vote for you, something that serves their interests. Just wanting to be on the Student Council isn't enough. Have one or two central issues about which you think you can make a difference. Maybe it's improving the cafeteria food or scheduling more school socials. Explain your stand briefly and precisely, and describe how you intend to fulfill your promises. *Don't* make promises you can't keep or that aren't reasonable, like a ban on homework, or you will lose your credibility.

67. State your experience. Your audience will want to know what qualifies you for this office. Describe any experience you have that you think would make you the best person for this job. Maybe you've held office before or had a leadership role in a school club or other activity and you think that background will make you a good Student Council member. Maybe you've worked cooperatively with teachers in another capacity, such as on the school newspaper. Don't brag about what you've done or go into unnecessary detail, but relate your qualifications succinctly and tell why they would make you the right person for this position.

68. Be positive. Build yourself up, but not at the expense of the other candidates. It's never a good idea to say mean or untrue things about your opponents. In general, people don't like negativity. It may even lose you votes. Focus on the good things you've done that make you uniquely qualified for this job.

69. An acceptance speech is a thank you. You may give this speech when you are elected or win an award or honor. It has a very direct purpose— to accept, in a formal manner, the award or position you've won—and for that reason your speech should be short and sweet.

70. Thank the people who matter. If you're accepting an award, you'll want to thank the people or organization that bestowed it on you and probably the people whose support and help made it possible. Some movie stars are notorious for running off at the mouth when it comes to thank you's on Oscar night, and they have to be cut off. Keep your list short—a teacher who encouraged you, a friend who supported you, a parent who believed in you. If you're afraid of leaving anyone out, just end by thanking your "family and friends."

They'll know who they are.

71.

Be gracious. When you make your acceptance speech, take a moment to mention the competition and compliment them. As the winner you can afford to be gracious. Next time, who knows, maybe the person who lost will be sitting where you are, and then you'll want him or her to say something nice about you.

72. An introductory speech is meant to introduce someone else. This is one of the rare times when you speak in public and the spotlight is on someone else, not you. So relax and enjoy your brief moment in front of the audience.

73. You must get the person's name right! To mispronounce the name of the person you are introducing is unforgivable. If it's an unfamiliar or difficult name, make sure you find out the correct pronunciation ahead of time and practice until you get it right.

74. After announcing the person's name, state his or her accomplishments. This shouldn't be a long list, just a few important highlights from his or her career. If possible, you might want to ask the person ahead of time how he or she would like to be introduced. If the person is receiving an honor or award, you may want to tie in other achievements that relate to this honor.

75. If the person you are introducing is giving a speech, include the topic in your introduction. You might also wish to include a sentence or two about why the person is speaking on this topic. Keep it brief. Let him or her define the topic further. The speaker is the one giving the speech, not you!

76. Get offstage quickly. When your introduction is finished, leave. If you are giving the person an award, present it, shake hands, and then get off the stage. Let the award-winner speak.

77. An announcement is brief and contains specific information. Announcements can range from "please observe the exit signs" to "come to our fund-raiser." You might be asked to make an announcement at your church or synagogue service, at a Boy Scout or Girl Scout meeting, or at a school assembly.

78. Speak loudly and clearly. Announcements are often made to large groups of people whose focus may be elsewhere. You may have to speak up more loudly than usual, even with a microphone, to get their attention. And speaking of getting their attention . . .

79. Use your imagination to make your announcement memorable. Let's face it: Announcements can be boring. How many times have you zoned out listening to your principal over the PA system at the start of the school day? If you are telling people about some activity that you are a part of—a fundraiser for your organization, for example—it's important that you sound like more than just an announcer. Be a salesperson delivering a pitch. The better your pitch, the more people will respond positively to the message.

80.

Come up with a clever opening. Openings of announcements, as in nearly all public speaking, are crucial to getting the audience's attention and keeping it. A little humor goes a long way to create a good opening. For example, let's say your youth group is holding a spaghetti supper to raise money for a trip. You might turn your announcement into a TV commercial:

"Are you tired? Run down? Never seem to have any energy anymore? Come to the Youth Service's Spaghetti Supper on Saturday and get a carbo rush that will put energy back into your sagging body!"

You can also use a visual aid to make your announcement more effective:

"They say a picture is worth a thousand words, so here's a picture you won't be able to resist. Looks good, doesn't it? Okay, and here are a few words to fill out the picture. . . ."

81.

Don't forget the facts! Those "few words" in your announcement should be the important details that everyone needs to know if they're going to show up at your function. They include:

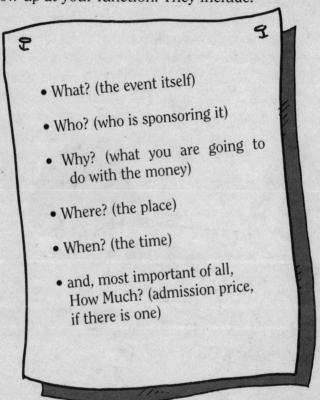

- What? (the event itself)

- Who? (who is sponsoring it)

- Why? (what you are going to do with the money)

- Where? (the place)

- When? (the time)

- and, most important of all, How Much? (admission price, if there is one)

Have all this information written out on an index card or a sheet of paper so you don't forget it. No matter how creative your announcement is, if you don't give all the information people need—or if it's not accurate information—your purpose will be unfulfilled.

82. An opinion speech is a personal opinion for or against something; it is usually delivered at a public meeting or public hearing. The yearly town meetings held in many small New England communities are examples of one of the purest forms of democracy on earth. All townspeople eighteen years and older get a chance to speak about public issues that affect their lives—and then to vote on them. You may not live in such a town or be old enough to give your opinion at a town meeting, but other kinds of public meetings invite citizens of all ages to speak out. Often a board of town officials will listen to each person speak and later make a decision in the matter, based in part on people's feelings and how well they were able to express their opinions.

83. Attend a public meeting just to see what it's like. You'll find out how important issues are discussed and resolved in your community. Pay special attention to the way that ordinary people are given an opportunity to voice their opinions, often lining up before a microphone to do so.

84. When an issue affects you or you feel strongly about it, exercise your power of free speech. Usually adults are the ones doing all the talking at meetings and hearings, but if the issue affects your school or the young people in your community—for example, the building of a recreation center or the much-needed renovation of a school—there's no reason why you shouldn't speak, too. If you're nervous about expressing your opinion in public, you may want to bring along a parent or friend for moral support.

85. Come prepared to speak. Each speaker gets only a few minutes at most of these meetings, so make an effort to prepare what you're going to say. Time your comments so you won't be cut off before you finish and hone two or three of your best points down to a few well-chosen words. It's probably a good idea to write down your speech on index cards or at least have some good notes.

86. Keep your remarks focused. Don't start bringing up other issues you feel strongly about that are not relevant. Stick to the issue at hand. Your words will have greater impact, and people won't dismiss you as a chronic complainer.

87. Don't get emotional. You may feel passionate about this issue, and that's good. But keep your emotions in check. Your arguments will be more forceful and effective if you stay calm and objective.

88. Don't get personal. Avoid attacking those who may disagree with you. Try to be positive and upbeat in your response. Make your case but don't go out of your way to make enemies.

89. Be community-minded. Too often people who speak out at public meetings focus entirely on themselves. It's okay to talk about how you are personally affected by an issue, but you should also make a strong case to show how the entire community is affected. This approach will strengthen your argument and will win more people over to your side.

90. Feel good about speaking at a public meeting. This kind of public speaking may be one of the few times when your words can really have a positive impact on your entire community. By speaking up you are being a good citizen and contributing to society.

Chapter 6

On the Spot:
Speaking Impromptu

Speaking impromptu means speaking on the spot, with little or no time to prepare what you are going to say. It is something many people are never asked to do in public and wouldn't want to do. If, however, you have done some public speaking and have done a decent job, you may find people turning to you when something needs to be said on a moment's notice.

There's no need to panic! The tips in this chapter will help prepare you so you will be able to speak at any time.

91. Your preparation for speaking impromptu is your past experience as a public speaker and as a person. The word "impromptu" comes originally from the Latin *in promptu,* which means "in readiness." Good public speakers are always ready—in the sense that they instinctively know how to phrase thoughts and to structure a speech with an opening, a body, and a conclusion. Furthermore, if you are asked to speak on a topic you know a lot about, you will probably have plenty to say. Even if you don't know a lot about a topic, you may have had experiences relating to that topic that will make your impromptu speech more interesting.

92. Often, a person is asked to speak impromptu at a social gathering, such as a birthday or anniversary party or some other celebration. It may be just a few words when you sit down to eat or before the presents are opened. A brief, entertaining speech can set just the right mood at a party or similar event.

93. When thinking of what you are going to say, try jumping to the conclusion. People aren't supposed to jump to conclusions, but it's okay when you're speaking impromptu. Why go to the end, when you don't even have a beginning yet? Because with the little time you may have to put your speech together, you need to think fast. And if you know where you want your thoughts to end, you should be able to fill in the rest quickly.

Here's an example: It's your best friend's birthday and his mother asks you to say a few words before the party gets under way. Your conclusion is pretty obvious. You want to congratulate him on his thirteenth birthday. Happy Birthday, Dan!

94. Find a way to make your opening fresh and interesting. Once you've decided on a conclusion, work backward to figure out what your opening will be. With a little thought, you can think of an opening idea that's lively and fun. For example, you might think that thirteen is an unlucky number. But it's not unlucky for your friend Dan, who is lucky in many ways. Now you've got some ideas to enliven your speech.

Here's one opening you might try out: "Thirteen is supposed to be an unlucky number, but I wish Dan lots of good luck on his thirteenth birthday."

95. Now move toward your conclusion with some details in the body of your impromptu speech. Ask yourself a question: Why is Dan a lucky guy? Well, he has great parents, lots of ability (enumerate a few of his talents), and he's got great friends like you (touch of humor). There's your body, leading up to your conclusion— Happy Birthday, Dan! Easy, huh? Now, give your speech. Then sit down, wipe the sweat from your brow, and enjoy the party.

96. Most impromptu speeches are short and sweet, so don't make a big deal out of it. Nobody's expecting you to deliver the Gettysburg Address here, just a few appropriate remarks for the occasion. Since the audience, knowing this is impromptu, may have lower expectations than usual, anything you do to rise above those expectations will be appreciated and applauded. And if you don't do so well, your audience will be quick to forgive you. It's basically a win-win situation.

97. Perhaps the best thing about speaking on the spot is that you don't have the time to worry. Speaking impromptu may actually be easier than preparing a speech in advance. Sure, you have time to figure out exactly what you're going to say for a real speech, but you also have more time to worry about it. There's hardly any time to worry when you're speaking impromptu, and this may actually make it easier for you to focus on what you're saying with a minimum of nervousness.

98. So the next time someone gets the bright idea of asking you to speak on short notice, think twice before you beg off, fake an illness, or run the other way. You'll be helping someone out, and you might just have the time of your life.

99. Now that you've learned all these things about public speaking, go out and try it! Take every opportunity you can to speak in public—at school, at church or synagogue, at organizations you belong to, maybe even at a public meeting. Remember—what you have to say is important.

100. The only way to get better at public speaking is with practice. Public speaking is like anything else you attempt—the more you work at it, the better you'll get. At first you may be overly nervous, make mistakes, and feel you could've done better. But the more you speak in public, the easier it will get. Gradually you'll feel more comfortable and sure of yourself, and you'll be more successful.

101. Reward yourself! Give yourself a treat after every speech. You've earned it!

Appendix

The checklists in this chapter offer quick reviews of some of the skills you've learned about in this book. Scanning the lists will help you prepare yourself for speaking in public.

Information about bibliographies is also included here to help you keep track of all the sources you use for your reports.

Tools You'll Need for
✔ Public Speaking ✔

____ pencils

____ pens

____ 3 x 5 index cards

____ spiral-bound notebook for taking notes

____ paper for outline and written report

____ research books, periodicals, and
       newspapers

____ tape recorder for interviewing people
       and recording yourself practicing
       your report or speech

____ non-print reference sources (such as
       videos, CDs, or personal interviews)

____ visual aids

Presentation and Demonstration:
✔ Checklist ✔

Ask yourself the following questions as you prepare your presentation or demonstration. Check the blank if the answer is yes.

____ Do I know the purpose of my presentation/demonstration?

____ Have I kept my presentation as simple and understandable as possible for my audience, breaking it down into easy-to-follow steps and defining any technical terms?

____ Have I practiced enough so I can talk and demonstrate comfortably at the same time?

____ Do I have everything I need before I begin?

Speech:
✔ Checklist ✔

Ask yourself the following questions as you prepare for your speech. Check the blank if the answer is yes.

_____ Do I know the purpose of my speech and the audience to whom I am giving it?

_____ Have I familiarized myself with the space in which I am speaking?

_____ If my speech is a campaign speech, have I taken a strong stand and stated it clearly?

_____ Have I been positive and stated my experience for this office?

_____ If my speech is an acceptance speech, have I briefly thanked the people who matter most and been gracious to my competition?

_____ If my speech is an introductory speech, do I know how to pronounce the name of the person I am introducing?

_____ Do I know enough about this person's background to pick out some highlights to include in my remarks?

_____ If my speech is an announcement, does it contain all the necessary information, and have I come up with a clever opening that will capture the audience's attention?

_____ If my speech is an opinion speech for a town meeting, is it brief, to the point, and focused on the welfare of the community?

Oral Report:
✔ Checklist ✔

Ask yourself the following questions as you prepare your oral report. Check the blank if the answer is yes.

_____ Have I chosen a topic that interests me and fits my needs?

_____ Do I know the purpose of my report and have I met it?

_____ Have I used *all* the resources available to me, not just the printed ones, in researching my report?

_____ Have I taken good notes on my research and developed a suitable outline?

_____ Have I written an interesting opening to my report that will capture the attention of my audience?

_____ Does the body of my report contain important information about my topic?

_____ Does my conclusion summarize the main points and arrive at a conclusion about the topic?

_____ Have I included audio and/or visual aids to make my report more interesting and colorful for my audience?

_____ Have I written my main ideas on index cards, using brief phrases and as few words as possible?

_____ Do I know my report well enough to be able to give it using only the notes on my index cards?

Ask yourself the following questions before you actually give your oral report. Check the blank if the answer is yes.

____ Am I dressed appropriately, with my hair combed and teeth brushed?

____ Do I have everything I need, including index cards and/or audio and visual aids?

____ Do I know how to operate any equipment I'll need, such as an audio cassette player or an overhead projector?

Impromptu
Speaking Hints

These general guidelines will prepare you for
making almost any impromptu speech.
Memorize them!

- Don't panic! If you're asked to speak
  impromptu, take a deep breath and start
  thinking.

- Jump ahead to the conclusion. If you know
  how you want your speech to end, it's easy
  to work backward.

- Make your opening fresh and interesting.
  Begin with a joke or a brief story relating to
  the situation.

- Fill in the middle. Now's the time to be
  creative! Think of a few words that will link
  the opening and the conclusion.

Assignment Planner

When your teacher gives you a public speaking assignment—a book review, presentation, or demonstration—don't wait until the last minute to begin working. Use this helpful planner to get organized!

Assignment: _____

_____

Due Date: _____

_____

Type of Public Speaking: _____

_____ book/topic report

_____ presentation

_____ demonstration

_____ speech

_____

Length of Speaking Time (in minutes): _____

_____

Written Version Due Date: _____

Topic: _____

_____

Title of Your Talk: _____

_____

Main Ideas to be Presented:

1.

2.

3.

Visual Aids:

Audio Aids:

School Equipment Needed:

Bibliography Hints

If your teacher requires a written version of your oral assignment, you will need to list all of the sources from which you gathered information. Even if you don't have to submit a written report, your teacher may still want a list of the sources you used. The easiest way to keep track of all the books, periodicals, and other reference materials is to make a note of each source while you are looking at it. The basic information you'll need for books and periodicals is listed on the next page—along with a few samples of how the details for each of these references should be organized. Pay special attention to the punctuation of each type of entry.

Quick tip: The entries in a bibliography are always listed in alphabetical order by the author's last name.

Books:

Author's name, title of the book, place of publication, publisher's name, date of publication (You can find the publication information on the book's copyright page.)

Dahl, Roald. *Charlie and the Chocolate Factory.* New York: Puffin, 1964.

Fleischman, Sid. *The Whipping Boy.* New Jersey: Troll Communications, 1987.

Periodicals:

Author's name, title of article, title of periodical, issue information (volume, issue number, date), page reference

---

Franklin, John. "My Dog Is My Best Friend." *Pet Weekly* 12 (March 1997): 12–13.

Trautman, Mike. "Is Your Dad an Alien?" *Outer Space Quarterly* 2 (summer 1998): 64–67.

Copy these bibliography cards before you begin a report and use one card for each reference source. Be sure to keep the cards all together in a safe place.

Book Bibliography Card
Author's name:
Title of book:
Place of publication:
Publisher's name:
Date of publication:

Book Bibliography Card
Author's name:
Title of book:
Place of publication:
Publisher's name:
Date of publication:

Periodical Bibliography Card

Author's name:

Title of article:

Title of periodical:

Volume number:

Issue number:

Date of publication:

Page reference:

Periodical Bibliography Card

Author's name:

Title of article:

Title of periodical:

Volume number:

Issue number:

Date of publication:

Page reference:

Index

Look for all the books in the

101
Ways
series

101 Ways to Do Better in School
0-8167-3285-X $2.95 U.S. / $4.25 CAN.

101 Ways to Get Straight A's
0-8167-3565-4 $2.95 U.S. / $4.25 CAN.

101 Ways to Boost Your Writing Skills
0-8167-3835-1 $2.95 U.S. / $4.25 CAN.

101 Ways to Boost Your Math Skills
0-8167-3836-X $2.95 U.S. / $4.25 CAN.

101 Ways to Take Tests with Success
0-8167-4225-1 $2.95 U.S. / $4.25 CAN.

101 Ways to Read with Speed and Understanding
0-8167-4226-X $2.95 U.S. / $4.25 CAN.

101 Ways to Boost Your Science Skills
0-8167-4451-3 $2.95 U.S. / $4.25 CAN.

101 Spelling Traps and How to Avoid Them
0-8167-4923-X $2.95 U.S. / $4.25 CAN.

101 Ways to Speak in Front of Your Whole Class
0-8167-4917-5 $2.95 U.S. / $4.25 CAN.

101 Key SAT Words
0-8167-4938-8 $2.95 U.S. / $4.25 CAN.

Do you have a minute?

Then take the *One-Minute Challenge*. These books are packed with tricky challenges to test your basic skills in math, English, and vocabulary. With answers in the back of each book, these quizzes are a perfect primer for the SATs. Earn better grades starting today!

One-Minute Challenges: Math
0-8167-4077-1 $2.95 U.S. / $4.25 CAN.

One-Minute Challenges: English
0-8167-4076-3 $2.95 U.S. / $4.25 CAN.

One-Minute Challenges: Vocabulary
0-8167-4227-8 $2.95 U.S. / $4.25 CAN.

One-Minute Challenges: Math and Reasoning
0-8167-4228-6 $2.95 U.S. / $4.25 CAN.

Notes

Notes